Children of NORTHERN IRELAND

THE WORLD'S CHILDREN

Children of
NORTHERN IRELAND

MICHAEL ELSOHN ROSS
PHOTOGRAPHS BY FELIX RIGAU

Carolrhoda Books, Inc./Minneapolis

To all the wonderful children we met in Northern Ireland and their dream of a peaceful future.
—*M. E. R. & F. R.*

The author and photographer would like to acknowledge the staff and students of Saints and Scholars Integrated Primary School, Bushmills Primary School, Cullycapple Primary School, Portora Royal School, Moyle Primary School, and St. Eugene's Cathedral. Many thanks to the families of the children who appeared in this book for their enthusiasm, hospitality, and help in reviewing the manuscript.

Text copyright © 2001 by Michael Elsohn Ross
Photographs copyright © 2001 by Felix Rigau
Map on p. 7 by John Erste, © 2001 by Carolrhoda Books, Inc.

All rights reserved. International copyright secured. No part of this book may be reproduced, stored in a retrieval system, or transmitted in any form or by any means—electronic, mechanical, photocopying, recording, or otherwise—without the prior written permission of Carolrhoda Books, Inc., except for the inclusion of brief quotations in an acknowledged review.

Carolrhoda Books, Inc.
A division of Lerner Publishing Group
241 First Avenue North
Minneapolis, MN 55401 U.S.A.

Website address: www.lernerbooks.com

LIBRARY OF CONGRESS CATALOGING-IN-PUBLICATION DATA

Ross, Michael Elsohn, 1952–
    Children of Northern Ireland / Michael Elsohn Ross ; photographs by Felix Rigau.
        p. cm. — (The world's children)
        Includes index.
    Summary: Introduces the history, geography, and culture of Northern Ireland through the daily lives of children who live there.
        ISBN 1-57505-433-7 (lib. bdg. : alk. paper)
    1. Northern Ireland—Juvenile literature. 2. Children—Northern Ireland—Juvenile literature. [1. Northern Ireland—Social life and customs.] I. Rigau, Felix, ill. II. Title. III. World's children (Minneapolis, Minn.)
    DA990.U46 R664   2001
    941.6—dc21   99-050654

Manufactured in the United States of America
1 2 3 4 5 6 – JR – 06 05 04 03 02 01

It's not easy to plan a picnic in Northern Ireland, where the weather changes from hour to hour. Dark clouds can sweep quickly across the sky, bringing rain to the lush, green land.

Seana and her friend Gemma like to picnic in the graveyard at Layde Church, an old church that overlooks the Irish Sea. They eat sandwiches, soda bread, strawberries, and cookies. Then they play on the ruined walls and among the graves of drowned sailors and soldiers who were killed in battles of long ago. History is part of their everyday lives, as it is for many children in Northern Ireland.

Seana and Gemma live in Glenariff, a small town in a small country. Northern Ireland is about the size of the state of Connecticut. It occupies a small part of the island of Ireland. The rest of the island is a separate country called the Republic of Ireland.

Gemma and Seana rest against an ancient cross in the Layde Church graveyard.

Northern Ireland is part of a larger nation, the United Kingdom of Great Britain and Northern Ireland, also known as the United Kingdom or Britain. Along with Northern Ireland, Britain includes the countries of Scotland, Wales, and England.

Northern Ireland has not always been separate from the rest of the Irish island. More than a thousand years ago, the island was divided into small kingdoms called *tuatha*. Each tuatha had its own chief, but the Irish all shared the Gaelic language, the Roman Catholic religion, and many traditions.

In the 1000s, the tuatha agreed to follow a single king, Brian Boru, who helped them drive away Viking raiders. Then, in 1171, England's King Henry II sent his army to invade the island. Ireland slowly came under English control. Many English people settled and built their lives there.

Northern Ireland is divided into six counties. About 1,700,000 people live there.

7

The 1530s brought an even bigger change to Ireland. King Henry VIII left the Roman Catholic Church. He started the Anglican Church and made it England's official religion. This church and others that split away from Catholicism are called Protestant churches.

Henry VIII and most of the rulers who came after him wanted Ireland to be Protestant, even though the Irish wanted to remain Catholic. The English rulers took land away from Irish Catholics and gave it to English and Scottish Protestants. Eventually, Catholics weren't allowed to buy land, attend universities, or vote. Most became very poor.

The Irish tried to regain control of their land for hundreds of years. At times, groups of Irish fought the British, but they never succeeded. Finally, in 1921, the British and the Irish agreed to divide the island of Ireland in two.

The city of Armagh has two churches called the Cathedral of St. Patrick. One is Catholic (above, far right), *and the other is Protestant* (right). *Both were named for the missionary who built Ireland's first Christian church.*

The southwestern part of the island was mostly Catholic. It eventually became an independent country, the Republic of Ireland. But many Protestant families had lived in the northeastern part of the island for generations. They considered themselves British, not Irish. They didn't want to be part of an Irish country. So Northern Ireland remained part of the United Kingdom.

Since 1921, the people of Northern Ireland have struggled to live in peace. The population is about three-fifths Protestant and two-fifths Catholic. Many Catholics believe that Northern Ireland should become part of Ireland. But many Protestants want to remain part of Britain.

A few people on both sides of this argument are willing to use violence to get their way. They set off bombs. Sometimes they beat and kill those who disagree with them. Since the 1960s, more than 3,500 people have died in this conflict. The people of Northern Ireland call it "the troubles."

Graffiti on a building in Armagh supports soldiers in the Irish Republican Army, a secret army that opposes British rule.

Students at Saints and Scholars play Irish music.

Graeme and Denis live in the southern city of Armagh. When they were babies, the troubles were terrible. Armagh was home to constant fighting between Catholics and Protestants. Children of the two faiths attended separate schools and lived in separate neighborhoods. Although many people wanted the fighting to stop, most thought it never would.

Graeme is Protestant, and Denis is Catholic. Their parents and a group of other adults decided to bring children of different religions together. Maybe that way they could help stop the violence.

They started the Saints and Scholars Integrated Primary School, which is open to children of all faiths. The children of Saints and Scholars play and learn together. They even sing in choirs at each other's churches.

Although Denis and Graeme's families belong to different faiths, the boys have become best friends. They like to sleep over at each other's houses. On weekends, they sometimes go to car rallies, where they watch Graeme's dad race. In the school show at the end of the year, the boys sing a silly song with a heavy Irish accent. They do their best to please the crowd.

Above: *Denis* (right) *and his friend Neil perform in the school show.*
Right: *Graeme and Denis sing for the crowd.*

11

Joseph pretends to be an animal statue in the garden at Mount Stewart.

In most parts of Northern Ireland, Protestants and Catholics usually don't live in the same neighborhoods or go to the same schools. Joseph, who lives on the Ards Peninsula in county Down, travels many miles to attend a Catholic school. His father is a gardener at a large estate called Mount Stewart. Joseph and his family live in an apartment above the estate's old stable. There aren't many other children for him to play with, but he has a good friend who lives at the gatehouse.

Joseph likes to visit the estate's garden. Lady Edith Londonderry, who once lived here, created it almost a hundred years ago for her children. It contains giant statues of dodo birds, griffins, monkeys, frogs, and other animals, both real and imaginary.

Outside the gates of his home, Joseph bicycles on the cobbled yard where the carriages of lords and ladies were once kept.

Grand estates such as Mount Stewart were built on land that English rulers took from Irish Catholics hundreds of years ago. The new landowners made the Irish farmers pay rent to farm on the land. While the landowners lived in big houses, the farmers lived in small cottages on the worst part of the land. Life was difficult. Many farmers left Ireland for North America.

Ancestors of United States president Ulysses S. Grant lived in this farm cottage in county Tyrone during the 1700s.

On Northern Ireland's northwestern coast lies a city that has two names. The city's original name was Derry. That's what Catholics still call it. Protestants call it Londonderry, the name given to the city by the British. As in most Northern Irish cities, Catholics and Protestants live in separate neighborhoods.

Londonderry's older neighborhoods are covered with murals that express the beliefs of both Catholics and Protestants. Above left: Red, white, and blue are the colors of the British flag. They are associated with Protestants who want to remain British. Above: A mural painted in memory of Catholics who marched for their rights in 1972. Fourteen of them were killed by British soldiers.

Above: *Catriona plays the organ as the boys' choir practices.* Left: *Catriona and Colm in the cathedral*

Catriona attends church in Bogside, a Catholic neighborhood. She plays the organ to accompany the boys' choir at St. Eugene's Catholic Cathedral. Her brother, Colm, sings in the choir. Most of the boys live near the church, but many arrive late for practice. Father Martin scolds them gently. After practice, everyone files into the cathedral to perform the morning Mass. Catriona plays confidently, and the boys' clear, sweet singing fills the cathedral.

In Northern Ireland, music is an important part of family and community life. At school, Catriona plays the violin in a *ceili* band, which performs traditional Irish dance music. She also studies piano. At home she and her younger sister, Nora, often sing together. When Nora was fifteen, she traveled with a choir to the United States. The singers were from both Catholic and Protestant parts of the city. The trip was part of an effort to promote peace between the two communities, and Nora made many new friends.

Above: *Catriona plays scales on her violin. Music is her favorite hobby, but she plans to study medicine when she goes to college.*
Left: *Nora*

Catherine and her brother Alan live on a farm near the town of Aghadowey. The farm has been in their family for many years — since their great-grandfather's great-grandfather came here from Scotland. In those days, the main crop was flax, a plant used to make linen cloth. Mills spun the flax into fine linen, which was sold all over the world.

In modern times, most of the local farmers raise dairy cows, grain for livestock feed, and potatoes for the kitchen table. One of Catherine and Alan's chores is to keep a close eye on the cows. Each day during calving season, they count the newborn calves to make sure none are lost.

Catherine and Alan watch over the cows. Besides feeding and counting the calves, they also help their father take care of the farm's equipment.

Above: *Cullycapple students tend potato plants in the school's garden (above right). The children also raise barley, flax, herbs, and flowers.*
Right: *Catherine and Sandra look for beetles in the pond.*

Catherine and Alan attend Cullycapple Primary School just down the road. Outside the school is a garden with a bird feeder and a pond. Not all of Cullycapple's students live on farms, and the garden gives them a chance to work the soil. Catherine and her best friend, Sandra, like the pond best. They have fun watching the tadpoles, water boatmen, and whirligig beetles that swim back and forth through the water.

Life on a farm is quiet, but a small island can be even quieter. Rathlin Island is about five miles from Northern Ireland's northern coast and nine miles from Scotland. Granuaile says that Catholics and Protestants get along with each other here. She thinks the island is too small for anyone to hold a grudge for long. People see each other every day, and they have to work together to survive.

In summertime, a ferry crosses between the mainland and Rathlin Island several times a day. In the winter, rough storms can make the crossing difficult and dangerous.

Rathlin Island is home to more sheep and seals than people. Fewer than a hundred people live here full-time. Granuaile and her sister, Taise, enjoy watching the seals along the shore near Mill Bay. Sometimes more than 40 rest on the shore, looking like fat torpedoes. The seals let Granuaile and Taise come close, and the girls recognize many of them by their distinctive markings.

Granuaile and Taise use binoculars to watch seals. Granuaile wants to be a veterinarian someday. At home she has three guinea pigs and 16 cats!

Ice cream mustaches on Ciaran, Cathal, and Robert mean one thing—sales have been good at their rainbow shell stand. The boys color shells with markers and sell them to the tourists who visit Rathlin. When they sell enough shells to fill their moneybox, they head for the only ice cream shop in town. On good days, they get to buy ice cream twice.

Most people on the island are related to each other. Cathal and Ciaran are brothers and distant cousins of Robert. Robert's family has lived on the island for generations. Unlike most of the islanders, who are Protestant or Catholic, they belong to the Baha'i faith. Their religion teaches tolerance of all people's beliefs.

Ciaran, Cathal, and Robert work hard at coloring shells.

Left: *Cathal and Robert take a break.* Above: *The colorful products of the rainbow shell stand*

Sean and Fergus show off their miniature yachts. Sean's yacht is decorated with a shamrock, a traditional symbol of Ireland.

Sean and Fergus proudly continue a Rathlin Island tradition. More than 150 years ago, people began racing miniature yachts on Rathlin. The racing died out for a few decades but was revived by the island's priest, Father MacAteer. With some help from adults, Sean and Fergus built a pair of 22-inch-long, five-foot-high yachts. One year Sean came in second in the adult race! Both boys have won first place in the youth races.

It might seem like people would get bored on a small island, but Sean and Fergus find plenty to do. They like to search the shore, where they've found everything from a soccer ball to a letter in a bottle from Scotland. The boys also have fun visiting the lighthouse at the west end of the island. The lighthouse is automated, so it doesn't need a keeper. But it sometimes needs to be repaired, which is Sean's father's job. The lighthouse has saved many ships from crashing into the rocky cliffs.

The rocky shores of Rathlin Island can be dangerous for ships.

Fergus and Sean visit Sean's father at the lighthouse.

25

From the lighthouse, the boys can see the island's bird sanctuary, where thousands of birds are protected by law. Kittiwakes, guillemots, puffins, and other birds nest in the high cliffs during the early summer. Fergus's uncle, Liam, is one of the sanctuary's game wardens. Once Fergus helped him count the birds. They found over 39,000 guillemots alone! Fergus hopes that when he gets older, he can be a game warden, too.

Right: *Fergus watches birds from the lighthouse.* Below: *Seabirds nest on the cliffs.*

Living on an island as small as Rathlin requires flexibility. Very few adults can manage with just one job, because many jobs are part-time. Sean's father fishes in addition to his work at the lighthouse. Sean has many summer jobs, too. Besides helping his father at the west lighthouse, he sometimes joins him in lobstering. Sean also mows the lawn at the east lighthouse.

Sean earns spending money by mowing the lawn at the east lighthouse.

Lauren (third from left) *chases the ball during a tough field hockey match.*

Across the sea from Rathlin Island, Lauren and her friend Lindsay attend Bushmills Primary School in a mostly Protestant community on the coast of county Antrim. After school, the girls sometimes play field hockey against teams from other schools. The players use hockey sticks to pass a ball down the field, toward the opposing team's goal box. When they get close, they try to make a goal.

After field hockey, Lauren and Lindsay go to a bike safety class at school. A course has been painted on the blacktop in front of the school. It looks like a network of streets complete with intersections and stop signs. After days of practice, the children are ready to be tested by a road safety official. Each student must make proper turns, including hand signals. Lindsay wobbles a bit making a right turn, but she and Lauren both pass the test. The girls can ride their bikes on their own to the ice cream shop or each other's houses.

Left: *Lindsay concentrates on following the course.* Above: *A road safety official grades Lauren on her hand signals.*

The Giant's Causeway is made up of about 40,000 basalt columns. The tallest columns are about 40 feet high.

Another great place to bike is the Giant's Causeway. This strange rock formation is located on the tip of Northern Ireland closest to Scotland. It looks like a pathway of columns that leads across the water. An Irish legend says that a giant named Finn MacCool built the causeway so he could visit a lady giant in Scotland. Another story says Finn wanted to fight a Scottish giant who had insulted him.

The causeway's columns were formed millions of years ago, when lava oozed out of volcanoes and cooled into a type of rock called basalt. The unusual rocks attract thousands of visitors each year.

Mr. Bell's students visit the Giant's Causeway from Larne, a town farther south on the Antrim coast. The students learn about the causeway from Hill Dick, a naturalist. He shows them rocks shaped like camels and Finn MacCool's boot. The children also find colorful plants called lichens, pretty opals, and rocks that break apart in their hands.

Children from Larne learn about the causeway's natural history.

Left: *Jack at Turnley's Tower.*
Below: *Surrounded by shops, cars, and a telephone booth, the prison has become part of a modern town.*

Jack rests against the wall of Turnley's Tower, a 200-year-old prison in Cushendall. The prison was built by a rich landowner. In the 1800s, farmers who failed to make their rent payments were locked away here. The landowner poured hot oil on anyone who tried to rescue them. For Jack, though, the former prison is just one of many fun places to visit. It's on the way to the beach, where he plays in the sand and waves of the North Channel, the water that separates Northern Ireland from southwestern Scotland.

Jack plays on one of the many beautiful beaches on the coast of Northern Ireland. Most of the year, the water is too cold for swimming.

Above: *The rich, lush grass of Antrim makes excellent food for sheep and cattle.* Inset: *A sheep crossing*

Cushendall is at the mouth of one of the nine glens, or valleys, of county Antrim. The glens are a patchwork of grassy fields separated by rock walls. Many sheep are raised here. Sometimes their herders take the sheep down or across roads to get to fresh pastures. Drivers must look carefully to avoid hitting sheep and cattle as they travel down the narrow country roads.

At Portora Royal School in Enniskillen, Ashley and Kyle compete in crew, or rowing, races in Lower Lough Erne. (The word *lough* means "lake.") All Portora Royal students are Protestant. But the school's crew team is open to boys from other schools and religious traditions. Ashley and Kyle race on eight-person boats with boys from the Catholic school in Enniskillen. They say that everyone gets along. They have to if they're going to work well as a team.

Left: *Kyle and Ashley with their rowing boat, which is called a shell.*
Above: *Rowing requires strength and determination. Some of the races are three hours long.*

Crew requires a lot of practice. As the boats skim across the water, the eight rowers listen carefully to the coxswain. Like a team captain, the coxswain shouts orders such as "sharpen the catch," which tells the rowers to put their oars in the water. In a few weeks, the team will race in the all-Ireland championships in Cork, a city in the Republic of Ireland. During the two weeks before the race, they will practice twice a day.

Kyle follows the orders of the coxswain, who sits in the back of the boat facing the rowers.

Portora Royal is a school rich in traditions. It was founded by Britain's King James I in 1608. The walls are decorated with plaques honoring students from throughout the school's history. At lunch, the boys eat in the same dining hall where the writers Oscar Wilde and Samuel Beckett, two famous Portora Royal graduates, once ate. Classes are challenging, and Kyle and Ashley feel a lot of pressure to work hard. In both sports and school, they try to live by the rowers' goal, "Start fast and get faster."

Ashley and Kyle in their Portora Royal uniforms

Above: *Allison.* Left: *The abbey where Catholic monks once made their home*

On Devenish Island in Lower Lough Erne, Allison scrambles up and down the stone walls of a monastery built almost 1,500 years ago. Here lived Catholic monks who prayed, studied, and followed strict religious rules.

Allison and her family have come from nearby county Tyrone to show the island to relatives from the United States. Above them rises an 80-foot stone tower. Inside the tower, ladders connect one floor to another. Narrow windows overlook the lake. Long ago, monks looked out these windows, scanning the lake for the ships of Viking raiders. During raids, the monks hid inside the tower with religious books and other treasures.

Devenish Island's stone tower was built in the 1100s.

Like many Irish people, Peter enjoys eating chips, or fried potatoes.

Peter lives in the country outside Dungiven, a small town near Londonderry. Unlike many schools in the area, Peter's school is open to all religions. Though he is Catholic, all of his good friends at school happen to be Protestant. But the troubles have still affected Peter's life. Once, a Protestant church was burned in Dungiven. Peter couldn't understand why anyone would do such a thing.

On weekends, Peter often crosses the border into the Republic of Ireland, where his grandparents live. When he was younger, British soldiers patrolled parts of Northern Ireland to help control the troubles. Peter and his family had to pass through an army checkpoint to leave the country. Peter says it still feels strange to visit his grandparents without having to check in with British soldiers.

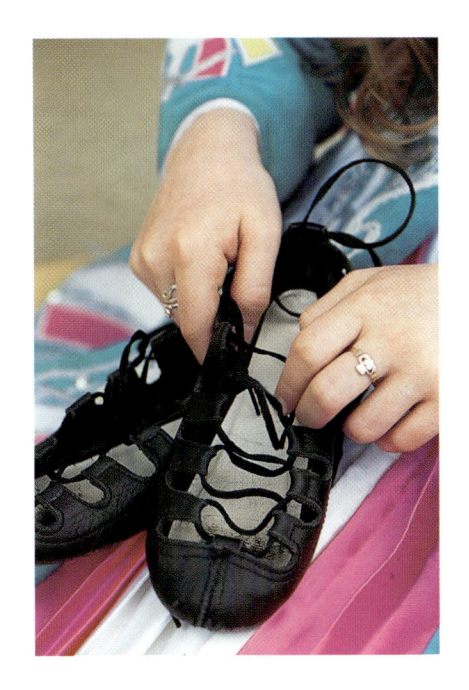

Left: *Dance is a tradition in Laura's family. Her grandmother has won prizes for her performances.* Far left: *Laura's dancing shoes*

Peter's sister, Laura, has been taking traditional Irish dance classes for three years. During the early centuries of Britain's rule over Ireland, Irish dance and music were banned. People weren't even supposed to speak the Gaelic language. But the Irish kept their traditions alive in secret.

In modern times, classes in the traditional arts are popular among children in Northern Ireland. Laura performs jigs and reels at school and at competitions. For formal dances, she wears tap shoes, a specially made dress, and a pin of Irish design.

Belfast and its harbor, as seen from Adam's neighborhood. Shipbuilding is an important industry in Belfast. The famous ocean liner Titanic *was built here from 1909 to 1912.*

Adam with a rugby ball

Adam lives in Belfast, the country's biggest city and main port. From his neighborhood of Sydenham, he can see the harbor. Sometimes Adam watches the ships or takes the train to visit the city center, but he spends most of his free time playing rugby with his friends Michael and Paul. Rugby is a rough sport somewhat like American football. Players must be able to kick, run, and tackle. On rainy days, the boys often come home muddy.

Adam plays rugby with Michael and Paul. Michael once kicked the ball so hard that it went through the window of a neighbor's camper.

Adam's mother grew up in Belfast's Shankill neighborhood during a time when there was a lot of violence between Catholics and Protestants. People on both sides of the conflict were beaten, and bombs exploded in stores and restaurants. Adam's grandparents still live in Shankill, but his parents wanted their children to grow up in a safer place. So they moved to Sydenham, a Protestant neighborhood.

Adam grew up watching the troubles on the television news, but contact with Catholics was not part of his life. Then, when he was 10 years old, he was chosen to perform in a television advertisement for peace in Northern Ireland. The ad told the story of two boys, one Catholic and one Protestant, who become friends.

As Adam acted with Henry, the Catholic boy in the ad, they really did become friends. Henry was Adam's first Catholic friend. Adam had never even visited a Catholic neighborhood until he went to Henry's home on Ormeau Road.

Adam at home with his sisters, brother, and grandparents

Years later, the boys are still friends. They go to the movies, go bowling, and play football (the sport Americans call soccer). Their families, like many others in Northern Ireland, hope for peace. They see Northern Ireland as a beautiful place where people can learn to live together.

Friendships like Henry and Adam's are breaking down old hatreds and shaping a future in which people will respect each other's differences. One day, perhaps Adam and Henry will be able to live in the same neighborhood without fear of violence.

In this poster from the peace advertisement Adam and Henry starred in, the boys walk together on a beach, friends for life.

45

Pronunciation Guide

Aghadowey   ag-uh-DOO-ee
Armagh   AHR-mah
Cathal   KA-huhl
Catriona   kuh-TREE-nuh
ceili   KAY-lee
Ciaran   KEER-ahn
Gaelic   GAY-lik
Gemma   JEM-uh
Granuaile   GRAHN-yuh
lough   LAHK
Seana   SHAHN-uh
Taise   TAYS
tuatha   TOO-ruh

Index

Aghadowey, 18
Animals, 18, 21, 26, 34
Antrim, county, 28, 31, 34
Ards Peninsula, 13
Armagh, 10

Baha'i religion, 22
Beaches, 32
Belfast, 42, 44
Bicycling, 29
Britain, 7, 9
Bushmills, 28

Catholic religion, 7, 8
Catholics, 7, 9, 10, 13, 15, 16, 20, 22, 35, 38, 40, 44
Ceili bands, 17
Churches, 6, 16, 40
Clothing, traditional Irish, 41
Crew, 35–36
Cushendall, 32, 34

Dance, 17, 41
Derry. *See* Londonderry
Devenish Island, 38–39
Down, county, 13
Dungiven, 40

England, 7, 8
Enniskillen, 35

Farmers and farms, 14, 18, 19, 32
Field hockey, 28

Finn MacCool, 30, 31
Fishing, 27
Food, 6
Football, 45

Gaelic language, 7, 41
Gardens, 13, 19
Giant's Causeway, 30
Glenariff, 6
Glens, 34

Henry VIII, King, 8
Henry II, King, 7
History, 7–9, 14, 38–39

Ireland, island of, 6-9
Ireland, Republic of, 6, 9, 36, 40
Irish Sea, 6

James I, King, 37
Jobs, 25, 27

Land, 8, 14
Larne, 31
Lighthouses, 25
Londonderry, 15, 17, 40
Lough Erne, Lower, 35, 38

Mill Bay, 21
Monks, 38–39
Music, 10, 11, 16–17, 41

Neighborhoods, 10, 13, 15, 16, 42, 44, 45
North Channel, 32

Peace efforts, 9, 10, 44–45
Protestant religions, 8
Protestants, 9, 10, 13, 15, 20, 22, 28, 35, 40, 44

Rathlin Island, 20–27
Rugby, 42

Schools, 10, 13, 35, 37, 40
Scotland, 7, 18, 20, 25, 30, 32
Ships, 42
Size, 6

Tourists, 22
Troubles, the, 9, 10, 40, 44. *See also* violence
Tyrone, county, 39

United Kingdom. *See* Britain

Vikings, 7, 39
Violence, 9, 44, 45. *See also* troubles

Wales, 7
Weather, 6

Yachts, miniature, 24

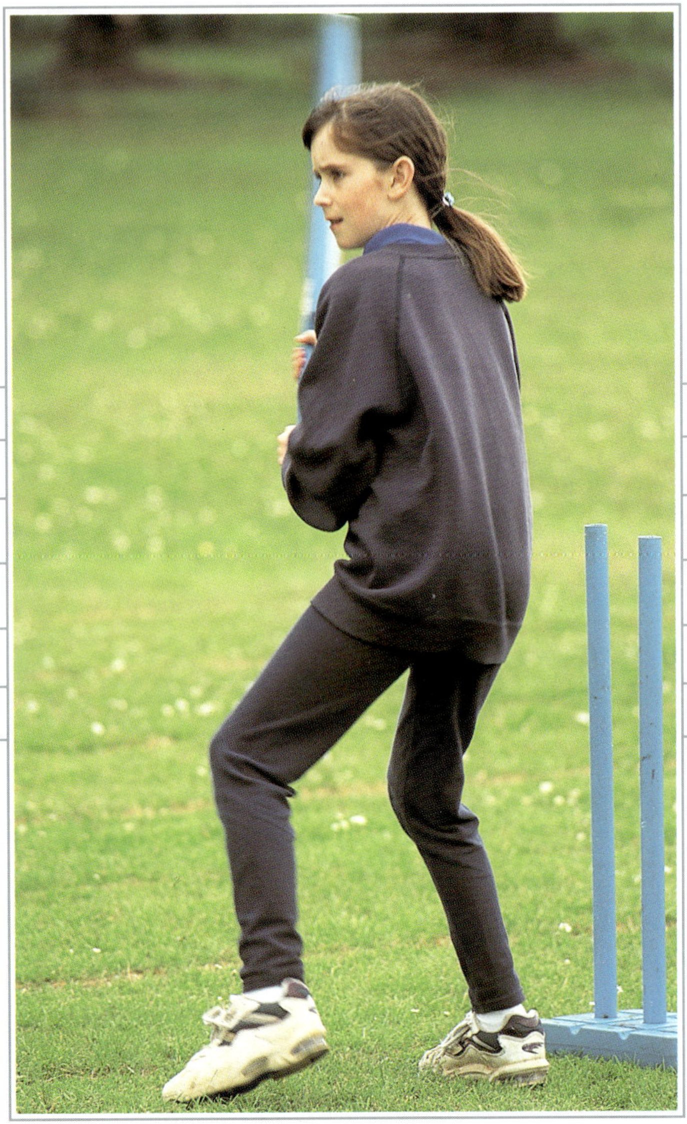